A Parent's Guide to Easy, Screen-Free Activities Children Will Love

Lorraine Allman

REVIEWS

"A brilliant book packed full of great activity ideas and helpful tips. Just what I was looking for!" **Rachel G**, parent

"I've just started to introduce some of the activities to my son, and he really enjoys them. Thank you so much for the stimulating ideas that I will continue to introduce to him." **Melissa R**, parent

"I have worked with young children for fifty years and have never read a book offering so much beneficial help to parents and educators." **Jenny Briggs**, International Consultant and Early Years Trainer [review of *The Can-Do Child*]

"Children don't come with a manual so the best way I have of supporting parents is to give them a toolbox and allow them to choose the right tools at the right time. For me, the way The Can-Do Child is being delivered provides parents with some really cool tools for their toolbox." **Dr Amanda Gummer**, UK's leading expert on play, play development, and child development [review of *The Can-Do Child*]

"As a family, the approach and activities are very, very special. They bring us together and make us actually appreciate, respect, and understand each other when you're trying to solve a problem or helping each other out on a path." **Caroline H**, parent

First published in Great Britain 2020
by Can-Do Child® publishing

ISBN 978-0-9957540-4-1

Dedication: for Dylan, so grown up but never too old to play

CONTENTS

Glass Half Full
Eat a Rainbow
Count and Catch
Blow bubbles
You are...
Let's Dance!
Do a jigsaw puzzle
Introducing Yoga
Chalk it up
If I were in charge...
Feeling charades
Amaze Me!
Wheel of Choice

Let's get together: *family fun*
Desert Island Disco
Don't touch the lava (with a twist)
Values Jar
Have a Bake-Off
Design a family coat of arms
Can you hear what I hear?
20 questions
Spell my Name
Explore your day in colour
Host a themed dinner party
Would you rather?
Pot goes the music
Animal Ark

Life Skills: *Day-to-day living and key skills*
Top Dog
Create your own currency
Tell me where to go
Savings and Targets
Skills Share
Pass it On

Take a role play
Escape Room
Practical Skills for Life
It's a Goal
Party, Party
Be a Happy News Journalist

Can-Do Kindness and Giving Back
20 ideas for random acts of kindness and giving back

Can-Do Eco and Outdoors
Tree wrapping
Shadow Art
Ten bottle bowling
Nature's Numbers
Be Plastic Clever
Sticky Art
Home-made pizza kits
Take the Tech Outdoors
Bringing the Outdoors In
Treasure Hunts with a twist
Eco-Bingo!
Go on a Litter Pick
Spray the Shirt

Lucky Dip Boredom Busters
37 ideas to go in the lucky dip boredom buster bag

Preparing for return to school
All About Me Bag
Back to school bingo
Something that makes me...
Same Difference
Countdown calendar

Any activities carried out with children may carry a degree of risk, and not all activities in this book will suit every child. The reader should use their own judgement regarding the age-appropriateness of each activity for their child. The author cannot be held liable for any accident, damage, loss, or injury of any kind sustained by participating in any of the suggested activities.

For ease of use the word 'child' has been used throughout but should be substituted with 'children' where that reflects your situation. Similarly, the word 'parent' should be interpreted to mean anyone *in loco parentis*.

INTRODUCTION

Not long into the 2020 Covid-19 lockdown, I noticed a huge increase in the number of parents looking for activity ideas and inspiration on my Can-Do Child© Pinterest boards. From Outdoors, Indoors, and Special Needs, to Literacy and Numeracy, STEM, and Wellbeing, the views for screen-free activity ideas were increasing exponentially.

As a parent myself I share the concern of many others, whether during a lockdown or school holidays, that we need to encourage children away from screen play; however, finding alternative screen-free activities they will enjoy can be a challenge.

Inside this book

The play ideas sheet I have been sending to parents every week have become so popular that many subscribers have been asking for even more ideas, and that is how this book has come about. In here, you will find:

- More than 170 budget-friendly, screen-free activity ideas for children age 3-11 years.
- Activity themes include health and wellbeing, life skills, words and numbers, eco and outdoors, and kindness
- A dedicated section on family activities for everyone to join in the fun
- Ways to help prepare children for their return to school
- Parenting tips based on the Can-Do Child® philosophy

A note about arts and crafts

I'm the first to confess I'm not really an 'arts and crafts' kind of person. Most of my attempts at these sorts of activities fall short of the often perfect photographs in books or posted online. My own son isn't a huge fan of arts and crafts either, so I got to thinking maybe we weren't the only ones, and this is why I have decided to think about all the other brilliant ways of enticing children away from screens, rather than relying on traditional art and craft type activities.

About the activities

The majority of the activities are screen-free, however you will find the odd one, especially in the STEM section, where technology is used to enhance or add value to the activity. This is a great way to show children the many ways in which technology can be used other than for playing games!

All the activities are quick and easy to set up using everyday materials and objects from around the home. The majority need little, if any, forward planning, but if you want to be organised then you could put together a box of resources using the list below. Don't worry if you don't have time for this, let your child take the lead and see how they improvise!

I'm confident your child will love these activities – some may be familiar albeit with a twist, others will be brand new. Whether you are looking for inspiration, need time to get on with your own work, or prefer a more planned approach to a screen-free activity programme, you won't be short of great ideas. Have fun!

Lorraine

The Can-Do Child®

Here are the main resources you will need:

Large piece of white paper
Crayons/pencils
Cling film
Sticky notes
Chalks
Paper clips
Cardboard
Ziplock bags
Paper plates
Empty jam jar
Wooden clothes pegs
Plastic bags

Coloured & white card and paper
Sticky back plastic (contact paper)
Sticky tape
Scissors
Rubber bands
Glue
Empty shoe box
Marker pens
Kitchen towel
Marshmallows
Kitchen towel cardboard tube
Toothpicks

Recyclable items such as empty milk bottles, bottle caps or jar lids

A WORD ABOUT SCREEN TIME

Although the majority of activities in this book are screen-free, that doesn't mean to say children shouldn't enjoy playing games on computers, smartphones, or tablets. The Can-Do Child® way is to make sure children have a balance of screen and screen-free activities.

Whether or not parents choose to restrict screen time for their children and by how much is a matter of personal preference, but there is plenty of research now showing that, for example, more than two hours of screen time each day can have a negative effect on children's health and wellbeing. So, how to go about achieving this?

The can-do approach to achieving a balanced screen diet involves all the family, starting with a conversation. Begin by talking about how technology and screens are all around us, but just as we need to make good choices about food for a healthy balanced diet, then it's important to do the same for our screen diet. Talk with them about what they think a reasonable amount of screen time is, then negotiate using questions to achieve an allowance you are generally happy with. If you decide to instigate a screen time 'allowance' then it should apply to all family members, with the various allowances displayed for all to see – being a role model is important here.

Next, think about how the screen time is to be balanced out. For example, you might decide that one hour of screen time is balanced with one hour (or even better, two hours) of activities away from the screen e.g. going for a walk, doing one of the activities in this book, playing board games etc.

It's important for children to develop their internal capacity to manage their own behaviour, so negotiating screen time allowances and sticking to them can really help develop their ability to self-regulate.

Younger children however will need something tangible to help them understand about limited time. Lollipop sticks or straws work well, where each straw or stick is exchanged for say half an hour of screen time. Remember to give encouragement and congratulate when children keep to the allowances agreed or make good decisions about screen time.

ACTIVITIES

1

ACTIVE WORDS AND NUMBERS

These activities are all about using words and numbers through games and in the everyday. Children will be developing their numeracy and literacy skills without even realising it!

Spot the Dots

You will need: Sticky notes, paper, marker pen

On a piece of paper draw squares with different numbers of dots inside. Next, write the number in numerical form from each square on a separate sticky note. Hide the sticky notes all over the house, or even in the garden! The goal is to find the sticky notes and match them to the dots in each square on the paper.

You can make your own set of dots or **print off the template at the back of this book**. This activity works equally well by substituting the dots with letters of the alphabet, and writing the letters on sticky notes.

The Objects of the Story

You will need: 5 or 6 random objects from around the house

Either you or your child selects 5 or 6 random objects from around the house. Now make up a short story to include each one. In fact, make up as many stories as you can!
Mix things up by writing down 'genres' or 'settings' on pieces of paper, fold them up and put them in a pot for the storyteller to select.

Genres may include: mystery, comedy, western, science fiction
Settings may include: the beach, fun fair, museum, haunted house
Make it even more challenging by adding a time limit in which to create the story.

Natural Maths

You will need: to keep an eye out for patterns!

In the house, garden, or out and about, look for shapes and patterns. Try to identify symmetry, fractals, concentric circles. Keep a small mirror handy to help. *Examples:* fences, leaves, pinecones, tree trunks, flowers, pipes, cut fruit, spider's web, butterflies.

We're Going on a Rhyme Hunt

You will need: imagination

Next time you're out on a family walk, take it in turns to say a word, then find something nearby which rhymes with that word. It could be an object or colour.

Here are some examples of rhyming pairs:

Tree	Plane	You	Jar	Cry	Glass	Frog	Dream
Bee	Drain	Blue	Car	Sky	Grass	Dog	Ice-cream

Book Bingo!

You will need: printed template at the back of this book, marker pen

A great way to encourage children to read in all sorts of ways!

Print out the template at the back of this book, or make up your own in discussion with your child – what new ways of reading can they come up with? Your child should cross each activity as they complete them over the Summer or within a timeframe agreed. A small reward for getting a 'full house' is optional but a nice surprise!

BOOK BINGO!			
Read in your **PYJAMAS**	Read to a **FRIEND** or relative	Read **3** days in a row	Find a **NEW WORD** in a book and learn what it means
Read a **NON-FICTION** book	Read in the dark with a **TORCH**	**SWAP** a book with someone-else	Read a book with a **NUMBER** in the title
Read **OUT LOUD**	Close your eyes and pick a book to read at **RANDOM**	Read a **POEM**	Read under the shade of a **TREE**
Listen to an **AUDIOBOOK**	Read on a **RAINY** day	Read in an **ACCENT**	Read a book which has an **ANIMAL** in the story
Measure your **TALLEST** book	Read a book that makes you **LAUGH**	Measure your **SHORTEST** book	Read sitting **NEXT to SOMEONE** who is also reading

Pasta Shape Sorting

You will need: a range of dried pasta shapes, muffin baking tray

Place a range of dried pasta shapes into a bowl. Give your child an empty muffin baking tray and get them to sort the pasta into shapes, using a separate space in the tray for each one. For an additional sensory activity, add in coloured pasta to sort, or dye your own dried pasta shapes (pop them in a ziplock bag with some standard tempera paint, shake around then tip out to dry for a few hours).

Tiddly Pom Poms

You will need: small pom poms (or similar small items), paper plates, wooden clothes pegs

On the wooden clothes peg, write a number your child is learning. Clip it to the top of a paper plate, then have your child count out the correct number of pom poms (or similar) on to the plate.

Make this more challenging by including addition or subtraction – e.g. they have one plate with 3 pom-poms, and one plate with 2. Clip a peg with the number '5' on it. How can they move the pom poms around so the total equals five?

Sort the Sequence

You will need: a range of different sized bottle tops or buttons

Mix up the bottle tops or buttons and have your child sort them into size from smallest to largest, then reverse from largest to smallest.

Make this activity more challenging by writing on numbers and mathematical symbols such as = or + then get them to put in number order, and create sums.

A Race Against Numbers

You will need: cardboard rolls, sticky tape, paper, pen, toy cars

Take a long cardboard tube (perhaps fix together two kitchen towel rolls) and place on a downward slant. On a long piece of paper mark out numbers from 1-20 as shown, keeping equal distance between each number. Gently drop each car down the tunnel, note where they land. Encourage your child to keep a record of the scores and which type of vehicles travel the furthest or least.

Box the Dots

You will need: template from the back of this book, or make your own; pencils

This classic game of joining dots to make boxes has been around a long time, but remains as fun as ever. **Use the template from this book** or make up your own. Each player takes it in turns to connect up two dots at a time using only straight lines (no horizontal lines). Keep going until your line makes a complete square then write your name in it. When no more lines can be drawn, the player with the most squares wins!

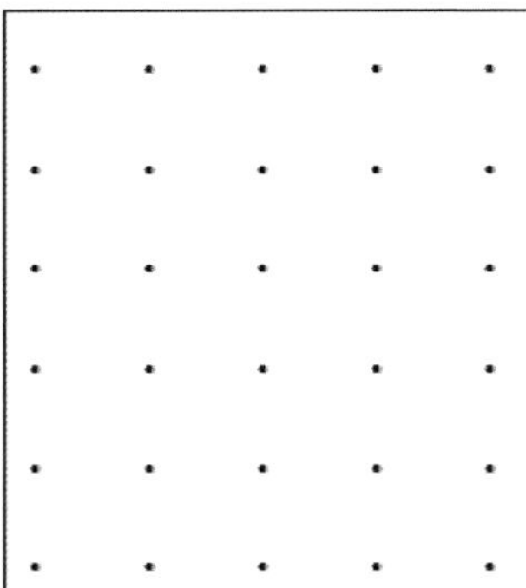

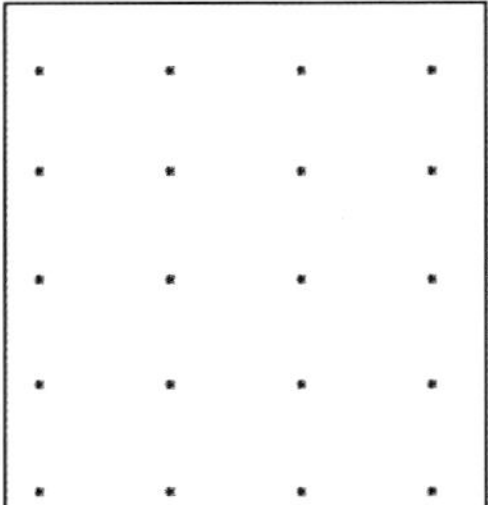

Be a Blackout Poet

You will need: an old book or magazine

This is a really fun way to get children using words to create art. In its simplest form, just choose a page of an old book (preferably one you don't mind being written in), select a paragraph and start to black out words with a marker pen. Leave behind words to create a new sentence or piece of prose.

More creative flair can be added to this activity by creating shapes and patterns through blacking out larger chunks of words. Go create!

How Many Hands?

You will need: piece of paper and a pencil

Have your child draw around their own hand and yours. Cut out the shapes then walk around the house measuring 'how many hands' particular objects are, comparing the difference between adult and child sized hands.

"The prime purpose of being four is to enjoy being four - of secondary importance is to prepare for being five." Jim Trelease

2

LET OFF SOME STEAM...

These activities bring together science, technology, engineering, arts, and maths to help children discover and experiment. It's not just about building things though – there are activities which require observation, problem solving, and of course a little bit of technology!

Magic Milk!

You will need: shallow dish, food colouring, cotton bud, washing-up liquid, full-fat milk

This fun activity explores chemical reactions in a safe way.
Pour some milk into a shallow dish, then put a few drops of different food colourings onto the milk. Dip the cotton bud into the washing-up liquid, then dab it onto the coloured milk in various places and watch the magic!

The science behind this is that soap is reacting with the fat in the milk, making the fat molecules move around- this is what happens when washing up dirty pans and how the grease comes off!

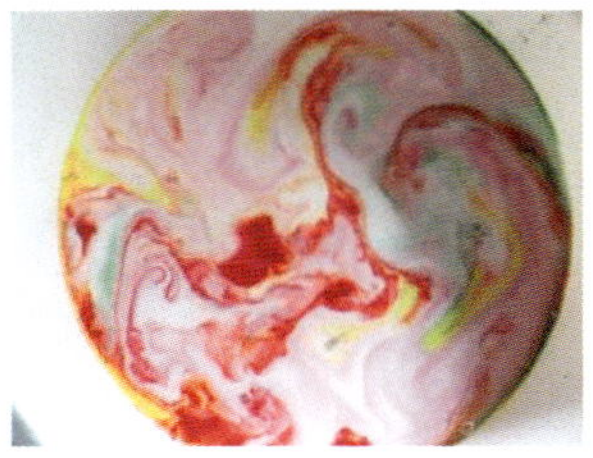

Moving Machines

You will need: observation skills and a notepad

Look around in the house or outside on a walk to discover objects which move through force. This could be through a variety of ways such as pushing, pulling, levers, gears etc.

How many moving machines can you discover? Here are a few to start you off:

Bicycle (gears and pedals); Car (engine); See-saw in a playground, Opening and closing a door; Going down a slide; Lid of a jar; Scissors; Stapler.

Block Challenge

You will need: Lego® bricks or similar, a challenge sheet printable

There are plenty of free Lego® challenge sheets available to download online, or you could just make one yourself based on particular themes related to what your child enjoys. They could have a daily or weekly challenge which may include building animals, robots, bridges, objects that float, things which fly, or even building whole cities!

Let's Make a Movie

You will need: smartphone or tablet, movie editing software

Making a film is simple using built-in software on a smartphone or tablet. **Create a short film** on anything of interest to your child around the home such as how machines work, or nature in the garden. How about capturing moments when out on a walk, or if your child is feeling more ambitious make a longer movie all about their school holiday time.

Phenomenal Phenology

You will need: smartphone with free time-lapse app; lots of patience

Phenology is the study of how things in nature change over a period of time, for example the blossoming flower, a seedling growing into a plant, a tadpole changing into a frog.

All these things, of course, take time, so try choosing something which changes over a shorter period of say a few weeks or even a day. Firstly, decide what you're going to study, then download a free app onto the smartphone such as *Lapse it*, *Time lapse*, or *Pic Pac Stop*. Now take one photograph each day (e.g. just as the seedlings start to show), ideally around the same time and at the same angle and distance - you may need to use some kind of marker to help with this. Keep doing this each day until you have all the photographs you need to show growth and the plant has flourished.

Use your app to generate your time-lapse movie of a seedling growing into a plant or of a flower blooming during the day and closing at night e.g. Morning Glory, Californian Poppy.

Coming Into Land

You will need: paper, marker pen

Build a selection of different style paper aeroplanes, then draw an aeroplane landing strip on a large piece of paper and measure which plane designs travel the furthest.

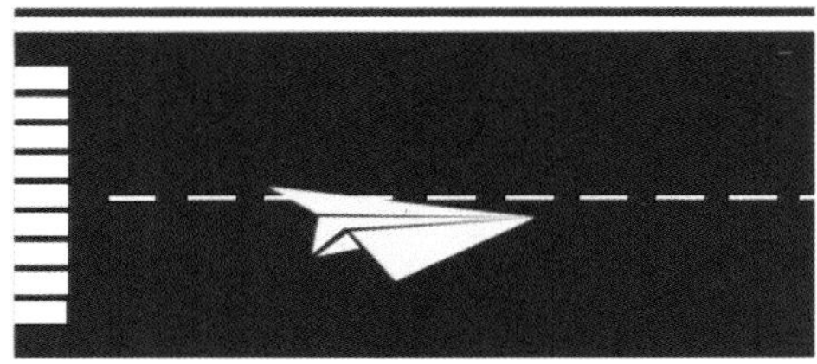

Balance Build

You will need: a range of uneven or oddly shaped items

Choose a selection of uneven items such as stones, pens, paper cups, plastic bowls, craft sticks, egg cartons etc. The challenge is to build a structure of any shape as high as possible using any, or all of the items they have to hand.

For a simpler challenge focusing on fine motor skills, build a tower or structure using just wooden toothpicks and small marshmallows.

Mess-Free Colour Explore

You will need: paints, ziplock bags, white paper, tape, glitter (optional)

Explore what happens when colours are mixed together - without the mess! Add one or two different coloured paints into a Ziplock bag, then tape it onto the table with a piece of white paper underneath.

Be sure to get all the air out of the bags.

Learn what new colours can be created by mixing two together, or add glitter to the paint for some extra sparkle, or just use glitter on its own in the bags to create interesting sparkly patterns.

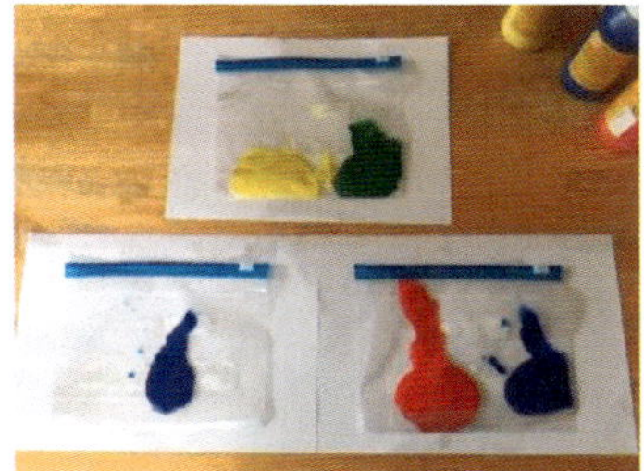

Digital Cloud Art

You will need: free drawing app

Lie back and look at cloud formations in the sky. Take digital photos of your favourites using a smartphone or tablet, then load those into a free drawing app such as *DrawIt!* or *DoodleBuddy*, then start creating digital cloud art. Share the photos with friends or create a montage and print out for display at home.

Magnetic Magic!

You will need: a magnet, two pots

Choose a number of objects made of different materials e.g. plastic, aluminium, fabric, or steel, and place them on a tray.

Label one pot with a √ for magnetic items and the other **X** for non-magnetic, then give your child the magnet and encourage them to discover which items 'stick' to the magnet and sort them into the right pots. Use a range of items such as toy cars, money, bottle tops, crayons, scissors, paper clips, pegs, nuts and bolts, cutlery etc. For a less structured activity, walk around the house with the magnet to discover what is magnetic. Look at door closures, fridges, mirrors etc.

Inventors Toolkit

You will need: an empty box, useful bits and bobs for an inventor

First, find a spare box, an empty shoe box or old lunch tin with a clasp is good. Fill it with useful, age-appropriate items a little inventor would find handy, such as a small screwdriver, marker pen, paperclips, scissors, glue stick, pegs, glue gun, sticky tape, thread, rubber bands. Let your child help choose the items to include and design a label for the front.

Now they have their own toolkit, it's time to invent. Introduce the idea of inventing by encouraging your child to find out about an invention they regularly use such e.g. a light switch, door handle, or toilet flush. Now ask them to imagine they are an inventor – *What would they invent? What problem would it solve?*

If there are any old toys or broken items around the house you don't mind being taken apart, encourage your child to do just that – it will help them understand the different components needed to make things work, and they could keep some of the parts in their toolkit for future inventions.

Desert Island Rescue

You will need: sticks, stones, plastic bags, foil, cardboard

Imagine you're trapped on a desert island. List out what you will need to survive until rescued using only what you can find on the island, and get to work on them. Here are a few suggestions:

Sundial: make one from seashells and a stick

Rope: Cut plastic bags into strips. Take two strips and start plaiting together as tightly as possible. Add more strips for a stronger rope.

Solar cooker: Using cardboard and foil, make your own solar cooker and try out with marshmallows on a sunny day.

Solar still: essential for filtering sea water

Water Parachute

You will need: balloon, plastic carrier bag

Fill a balloon just over half-full with water and tie the end. Now attach the balloon to a plastic carrier bag by tying the bag handles around the tied end of the balloon, then into a knot so it is secure. Throw the balloon up in the air and watch as the parachute inflates and brings it back down to earth. Experiment with different amounts of water in different balloons. Watch out for hard or soft landings too – the balloon may explode!

Magic Paper Towel Art

You will need: kitchen paper towel, marker pens, water

1. Take one piece of paper towel and fold it in half. Now cut this in half so you have two small squares, one behind the other, of the same size.

2. Take your marker pens and draw an outline of a picture on the top layer of the paper. Some of the ink will come through to the piece of kitchen towel underneath but that's fine.

3. Now fold back the top piece and colour in the outline on the second piece. A rainbow is one of the easiest things to draw to start off with.

4. Next, put some water in a wide bowl, then place the kitchen paper gently into the water. As the water soaks into the paper it looks like the colours of the rainbow have appeared by magic!

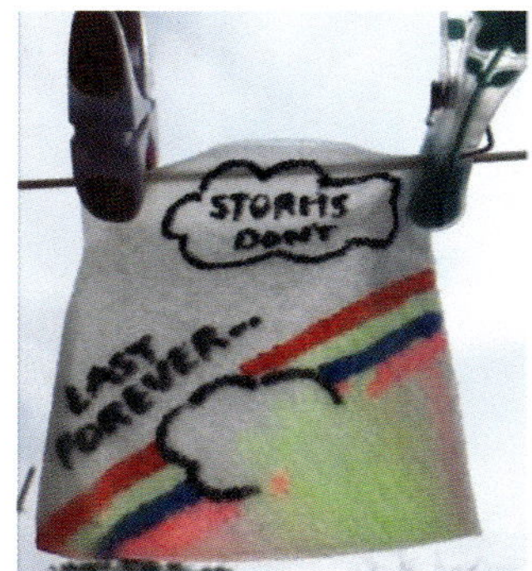

Children are far more likely to develop a can-do approach to life with a resourceful, resilient attitude, when they are given opportunities to explore and experiment.

Let your child take the lead in their play which will help them practice skills such as decision making and problem solving. It will also help them (and you) discover what interests them, and the pace at which they learn. Be sure to give them words of encouragement for effort, even when things don't quite work out as planned.

3

HEALTH AND WELLBEING

Staying active and healthy in body and mind is important for everyone, so we've put together a range of activities which will help you and your children do just that. From fun physical activities, to quiet down time and thoughtful conversations, try these ideas for positive health and wellbeing.

A Little Box of Calm

You will need: an empty box or two; age-appropriate items

Find an empty box (shoebox or similar is fine) and put together a selection of age appropriate items which your child can access for quiet play. Label the box 'quiet play' and make sure your child has a suitable space where they can sit quietly. Gather enough items in the box for them to be able to choose an activity.
Here are some suggestions:

colouring sheets and crayons * small puzzle * pieces of felt or other material cut into different shapes * small glue stick * sticky dots * blank paper * ruler * pipe cleaners * small paper plates * scissors * wooden pegs * marker/felt pens *

Glass Half Full

You will need: a glass half full of water

A half-glass of water is a lovely conversation starter with your child. You can begin by asking them whether they think the glass is half-full or half-empty. Explain it's not a trick question, as both can be true, but how they *choose* to see it can help them understand the different ways in which they may respond to situations they find themselves in.

For example, if something doesn't work out, they could respond by giving up and not trying again *(half-empty)* or they look for opportunities to try again and perhaps succeed *(half-full)*.

Be sure to keep the conversation going over time, noting occasions when a more *half-full* perspective could be beneficial, discussing ways to turn things around.

Eat a Rainbow

You will need: a list of the colours of the rainbow

When you next go shopping, give your child a list of the colours of the rainbow (like the one below) and have them tick off each one every time a food item with that colour is put in the shopping basket. Back home, plan and cook a meal which includes as many, ideally all, the colours so you can 'eat a rainbow'.

Colour	Name of food
Red	
Orange	
Yellow	
Green	
Blue	
Indigo	
Violet	

Count and Catch

You will need: ball and racquet

One player hits a ball into the air using a racquet. As the ball starts to fall, another player shouts out how many points the ball is worth. Whoever catches the ball wins those points. If, however, the person hitting the ball in the air tries to catch it and then drops it, they lose that number of points.

Take it in turns to hit the ball into the air, and call out the number value. The player with the most points at the end wins the game.

Blow Bubbles

You will need: bottles of bubble mixture

There are so many fun ways to play with bubbles – for younger children, they will enjoy crawling or walking, running around trying to catch or pop them, helping strengthen muscles and develop gross motor skills. Older children are more likely to want to try to see who can blow the biggest bubble which requires concentration on breathing and technique.

Simply watching the sunlight landing on bubbles creating rainbows, and how they silently 'pop' is also relaxing. Take a bottle of bubbles next time you go for a walk and share the enjoyment with others.

You are…

You will need: paper/card, colouring pens

Being able to give and receive compliments is an important part of both learning to support and encourage others, and build our self-esteem, so helping children understand how to do this from an early age is really important.

- First, you'll need to role model giving and receiving compliments and explain that it's a great way to pass on good feelings, costing nothing but a little thought.

- Compliments are a gift, so a great way to help teach this to children is have them **create a gift card** for someone they know - this could be a family member, friend, teacher. Talk about what they like about the person they're making the card for.

- For younger children, the focus initially is likely to be on things like what the person is wearing, but later you can help them move onto characteristics such as a smile or sense of humour. Give your child an introductory sentence such as "I really like your..."

I really like your garden...

Let's Dance!

You will need: paper, pen, music

Take it in turns to **plan a weekly dance class** for family and friends to join in. You could include relatives or friends who live away, but with whom you can connect remotely via Zoom or similar.

Put your ideas down on paper, think about what time of day it should run, how long it will last, where in the house you will run it, or perhaps even out in the garden! Work out the dance moves and how you're going to teach them – you could even make a poster to promote it. Don't forget to organise the music, and have fun!

Do a Jigsaw Puzzle

You will need: jigsaw puzzles

Quietly piecing one together on their own, or working as a team to create the finished version, jigsaw puzzles offer children a quiet activity whilst developing important key skills such as problem solving, and critical thinking. Taking time to think about and process shapes and possibilities, as well as for younger children developing their fine motor skills and hand-eye coordination, is important. If you don't have any jigsaws to hand, try a charity shop or create your own by:

- Baking a tray of biscuits, cutting them into different shapes and piecing them together
- Cutting out pictures from magazines stick them to card and cut into shapes to fit together

Introducing Yoga

You will need: a quiet and comfortable space

Summer is a great time to introduce yoga to children, without the structure and demands of school, and generally busy term-times, but how you introduce it will depend on their age, and whether it's also something new for you as a parent/guardian too. For younger children, keep it playful through animal poses, perhaps linking to a story book.

There are some great ideas for animal poses online. It's also fine to chat as you practice the moves, as well as making animal noises!

www.tomcorsonknowles.com

For older children, this might be an opportunity to have a conversation about what they think 'being healthy' means, practicing good habits now, not just when it comes to eating, but also physical and mental health, will form a solid foundation on which to build. Take a look online for ideas about introducing yoga at different ages.

Chalk It Up

You will need: chalk

Use chalk markings outside to play games such as hopscotch, bullseye, snail trail, and many more. Take a look at *Chalk Games on Pinterest* for literally hundreds of ideas. Have a go at creating a new chalk game too.

If I Were In Charge

You will need: imagination

Next time your child dresses up – as a king, queen, or superhero, ask them *"What things would you change if you were in charge?"*

This opens up a chance for your child to explore their hopes and dreams. Encourage them to move beyond "children could eat as many sweets as they wanted" and explore their innate sense of what is fair, the differences between right and wrong. Allow your child to give shape to their dreams, with the underlying message that the future can be shaped in large part by our dreams and ambitions.

Feeling Charades

You will need: cards from the back of this book, or make up your own

A card game with a difference:

1. Cut out the cards from the sheet **at the back of this book**, or make up your own.
2. Place all the cards face down, then take it in turns to take one and act out the feeling without saying any words.
3. The other person guesses what the emotion is.

Amaze Me!

You will need: selection of books/internet; paper; crayons

Choose a selection of books together or use the internet to discover more about a subject of interest to your child, have made history e.g. Banksy or Picasso for art lovers; Isambard Kingdom Brunel for railway and tunnel enthusiasts. Talk with your child about what these people have done, and what being 'amazing' might mean.

Now ask them to think about people who they've heard of or who they know. *Who do they think are amazing? What is it that makes them that way?* **Create a book cover or poster all about them**.

This activity can be extended by exploring with your child what they think they might do in the future which is 'amazing'.

Wheel of Choice

You will need: template from the back of this book to make up the wheel

Conflict can be difficult for a child to work through, whether sibling quarrels, or falling out with friends.

Make up this wheel from the back of the book to help them understand there are choices, and to navigate a positive way forward. If you're putting this together with your child, support them to come up with their own ideas to be included, which will encourage ownership of the wheel.

The key with this is to be clear that **the wheel *isn't about randomly spinning*** then trying out whatever idea the arrow lands on; they should keep spinning the wheel until they find a suggestion they feel happy to try out.

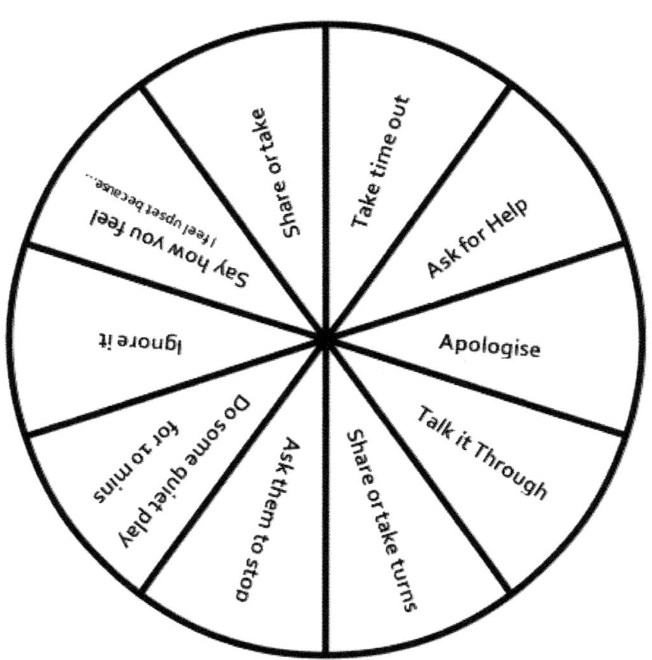

4

LET'S GET TOGETHER: FAMILY FUN

Whether your family is large or small, home provides a perfect, supportive setting for your child to learn and explore what it means to be part of a team, to engage with one another. Making time for fun and games together is really important, so try these activities whether you're at home, out in the garden, or on the move.

Desert Island Disco

You will need: music

Decide as a family what songs you would choose to play if you were stranded on a desert island. Put the playlist together, and hold your very desert island disco!

As an alternative, put together a playlist from the year that each member of the family was born.

Don't Touch the Lava (with a twist)

You will need: coloured circles of card (or cushions if you don't have card)

Place cut out, brightly coloured circles of card around the room. The idea is to move around walking only on the circles – everything else is lava, so watch out!

The twist comes when there is a race to 'rescue' particular items that have also been placed close to the lava – this might be words or numbers (if your child is learning these), or even food items which make up a favourite treat!

Values Jar

You will need: an empty jar; questions from the back of this book

On separate pieces of paper, write down lots of different scenarious or questions relating to social values that your child will understand or be able to have a go at discussing. **There is a list of ideas at the back of this book**. Fold each one and place them in your special jar.

Over mealtimes, or whenever the family is together and the time feels right, bring the jar out. Pass the jar around for everyone to remove a slip of paper, read it out loud, and give their response, followed by supportive discussion. Let older family members go first to model answers, and give your child plenty of time to think through their answers. If you prefer, just one question slip could be taken for everyone to answer.

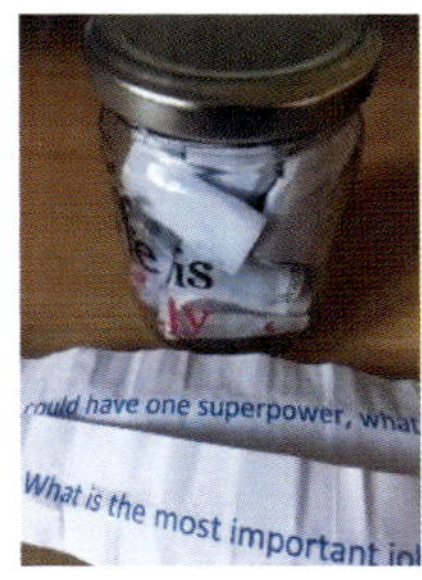

Have a Bake-Off

You will need: ingredients for your chosen recipe; timer

There are several ways to hold a family bake-off:

1. Decide on a recipe to cook, put the timer on, off you go!

2. Put some ingredients in a paper bag – chefs should invent a dish using those ingredients and cook it within 20 minutes.

3. Create a 'showstopper-style' dish of your own

You could have a bake off between siblings, or if there is one child, let the adults bake, and the child be the judge (marks out of 10 please!).

Design a Family Coat of Arms

You will need: paper and crayons

Talk about what your family motto might be, the kind of pictures it would contain, and colours, then get designing. Create and share with other family members. It could even become the logo for the family social media page!

Can You Hear What I Hear?

You will need: smartphone

Record lots of different sounds on your smartphone as you walk around the house, out in the garden, or go to the shops. **How many of these sounds can your child identify or guess correctly?**

Now show them how they can record their own sounds *(less expensive toy recording devices are available for much younger children)* so they can set the same challenge to another member of the family.

20 Questions

You will need: creative questioning

Decide on a mystery object, person, or place. Each player takes it in turns to ask a question to try to find out more information and help them guess the object/person/place. The answer can only be Yes or No. **A maximum of 20 questions** can be asked before everyone then has to guess (if they haven't already).

Spell My Name

You will need: observation skills

This is an easy and fun family game to play when you're on the move. Look for the letters in car registrations and be the first to spell out your name! If that's too easy, how about switching names and spelling each other's or taking it in turns to come up with increasingly more difficult words to spell.

Explore Your Day in Colour

You will need: observation skills

What colour is today going to be – red, blue, yellow, green? You decide! Now to explore your day in that colour... let's say you chose green, you could:

- Collect items from around the house which are green
- Eat green food
- Look for green insects or animals
- Take a photograph of green flowers
- Paint a green picture

Enjoy your day of colour. What colour will tomorrow be?

Host a Themed Dinner Party

You will need: imagination

Plan and host your own dinner party at home. This could be done as a whole family or let the children have a go! Themes could be based on animals, countries, people, or even a letter of the alphabet – think P for pasta, popcorn, pineapple, pies, potato, pesto.

Make up a menu, set the table, and decide on the music. Take it in turns to be waiter if there is more than one child, with older children helping to cook. Try a virtual themed dinner party by sending the menu and details over to friends or relatives and sitting down together (albeit virtually) to chat and enjoy.

Would You Rather...?

You will need: the list of question cards at the back of this book

Print out the list of **question cards from the back of this book** and keep them handy anytime you want a quick, fun game for everyone to enjoy. Take it in turns to pick up a question card. Each one starts with *'Would you rather...'* and gives two choices. The player answers the question, explaining why they gave the answer they did.

Older children can be challenged (constructively!) and you may well find that the conversation continues over dinner, in the car, or wherever you're playing the game. A great way to help children learn about decision making.

Would you rather...	**Would you rather...**	**Would you rather...**
Have an extra finger or an extra toe?	Eat a lemon or eat marmite?	Have wings or wheels?

Pot Goes the Music

You will need: a pot; paper and pen

This is a great way to start each day, and everyone gets to hear (eventually!) their favourite song. Each member of the family writes down four of their favourite songs on a separate piece of paper without anyone-else looking (you may need to help younger children with this).

Fold the pieces of paper up and put them in a pot (or jar). Take it in turns to pull a piece of paper from the pot each morning, and whatever is written on there is the song which will start your day!

Animal Ark

You will need: pictures of animals; sticky tape

This activity works best with lots of people so a family gathering, or party is ideal. Cut out pictures of animals, making sure there are two of the same. Show each player the animal they are going to be, then stick that picture on to their back. They should then move around the room and make noises just like their animal. The idea is for everyone to find the animal which matches theirs.

5

LIFE SKILLS

Holidays are a great time to help children learn basic life skills such as cooking, budgeting, washing, ironing, and DIY. As well as the practical, there are also other life skills to learn such as how to problem solve, be resourceful, resilient, and apply critical thinking. These activities will help your child develop all of those, and you may even find you have a little extra help around the house!

Top Dog

You will need: leadership skills

In this activity, your child gets to be the boss! It's for them to decide what chores need to be carried out and who does them. Give your child free reign, although younger ones may benefit from discussing and planning chores together as a family.

Your child will need to think about how to delegate tasks, consider strengths of others and may need to negotiate. They also need to be sure tasks are allocated appropriately so that they are achievable by, for example, younger siblings or less able members of the family. Are they showing consideration to others?

Take it in turns to be 'Top Dog' and talk about what lessons have been learned. Don't criticise or make comparisons, but explore ways in which everyone has a role to play in working as a team to get things done.

Create Your Own Currency

You will need: objects to trade with

Have your child devise their own form of currency which can be used for bartering at home. First choices will often be chocolate or sweets, but more tooth-friendly options are marbles, sparkly stones, or buttons. Alternatively, collect up to 5 possessions they feel have value or would interest other people.

Help your child assign 'values' to the currency and agree on what is to be 'traded', then arrange a trading time in which you all bring your goods; perhaps make it more formal by having soft drinks while you barter. Then start off the negotiations!

It can take time for children to learn the art of compromise, collaboration, and negotiation, so be patient. You may need to lead the activity to start with – explain what you have, its value, and what you would like to exchange it for.

Tell Me Where To Go

You will need: indoor or outdoor space; blindfold

A great activity at home or out and about. Set up a simple obstacle course, blindfold one player and the other calls out directions to lead them through the course. If playing outside then give directions to a particular place such as a park bench, or tree.

For younger children, model the activity so they know the directions and location words e.g. forwards, backwards, left, right, diagonal, to the left/to the right.

When completed or reached their destination, remove the blindfold, and talk about how easy or difficult it was to follow the instructions – what could have been improved or done differently? How well were the instructions followed?

Savings and Targets

You will need: 1 clear jam jar (or 3 if you do the extended activity)

Take one clear jam jar, draw a 'SAVE' label and stick it to the jar. Now help your child set an easily achievable target e.g. saving for a new toy or an activity they want to do. Help them work out how many days they think it will take to reach the target, then start saving regularly (perhaps earning money from helping out with chores around the house).

Give plenty of encouragement and praise as they save. This activity could be extended to include two additional jars with the labels 'SPEND' and 'DONATE'. Increase the size and difficulty of the target to save as your child's learning and understanding progresses. Bring saving into everyday situations such as when they see a new game they'd like – set the target as the cost of the game, then discuss ways in which they can begin to earn money to save for it.

Skills Share

You will need: a skill to share

Each member of the family (or just siblings) decide on a particular skill they have which they want to share with others. This could be an older child helping a younger one learn how to colour in pictures, teaching particular sports e.g. how to play football, or tennis, through to tying shoelaces, cooking, or use a computer.

Pass It On

You will need: items you no longer need or want

Holidays are a great time to de-clutter the home so get your child involved, and plan a garage sale, book a space at a local car boot, or give to charity. Sort the items into different piles such as repair, charity, sell, or throw away.

Explain the importance of keeping the *throw away* pile to a minimum – think environment, but also in value terms *one person's rubbish is another's treasure* - and help them work out what toys could be mended or cleaned and given to charity. Find out about local charities and what they need – they often put calls out for donations of clothes and toys for children.

Take a Role (play)

You will need: imagination and items from around the house

Pretend (or role) play activities are a great way for children to learn life skills. Get involved as the customer, though you may need to be flexible about what they 'stock' depending on what's around the house or in their toy box. Here are our top ten suggestions:

- Café (use paper cups, plates)
- Grocery Store (check in kitchen cupboards)
- Art Shop (paints, paper, brushes)
- Car Mechanic (collect toy car parts)
- Florist (make your own flowers, or pick from garden)
- Bank (real money to help children learn the value)
- Ice-cream parlour (pom poms are useful for this)
- Furniture shop (they could sell you your own sofa!)
- Garden centre (use plant pots, seed packets)
- Clothes shop (use theirs or your clothes and shoes)

Escape Room

You will need: to be thinking ahead

An Escape Room is one of the few activities in this book which does require a little forward thinking, but it's well worth it to see the whole family (or just the children) try it out. **Create a series of clues and puzzles which the team have to solve to 'escape' from a room.**

Set age appropriate clues, and if younger children find the idea of 'escaping' difficult, present it as a 'find the treasure' style activity.

Everyone will need to work together to solve problems, apply critical thinking, and communicate effectively to be able to escape. You could place clues in balloons which have to be popped, use invisible ink messages, and have a combination lock on a box to be opened. Take a look online for inspiration.

Practical Skills for Life

You will need: the list below – see back of book for full printout (or make up your own)

Holiday time provides a great opportunity for children to learn practical life skills – 'real world' things which will be useful for them as they grow up.

It's never too early to get them learning, but as much as we know it would be helpful for them to learn how to do the ironing or lay the table, do let your child choose what they want to learn first, and give lots of encouragement (even if it isn't quite how you would do it).

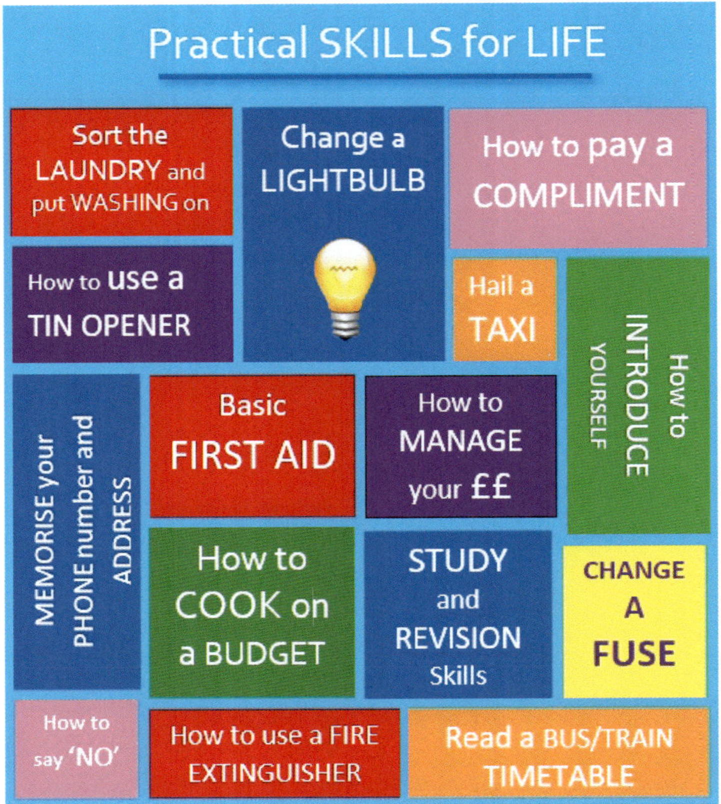

It's a Goal!

You will need: aspirations

Help your child set a simple goal based on what they would like to achieve over the Summer. This could be learning to ride a bike without stabilisers, learning to code, cook, anything they like.

Get them to write the goal down, then talk about what needs to happen to help them achieve it.

Make sure the goal is realistic – even older children can find targets and goals like a mountain to climb and that's the last thing they need over the holidays – it should be fun and motivating, so follow these top tips:

- Break the goal down into smaller steps
- Post up the goal (with steps to achieve) somewhere everyone can see – goals are more likely to be achieved if they are written down
- Encourage and support based on the effort they are putting in e.g. I can see you're really trying
- When achieved, sit down and talk through how they feel it went, what worked well and what could be done differently. Are there other things they'd like to achieve? How will they do that?

You may find the discussion leads on to broader talk about their hopes and dreams - just let your child lead, and listen, repeating to confirm that you have heard. Encourage other family members to write their goals down too. Post them all up in the house for everyone to see and support.

"If parents want to give their children a gift, the best thing they can do is to teach their children to love challenges, be intrigued by mistakes, enjoy effort, and keep on learning. That way, their children don't have to be slaves of praise. They will have a lifelong way to build and repair their own confidence."

Carol S. Dweck

Party Party!

You will need: party bits and bobs

Organise a party at home for the immediate family. Agree a small budget to buy items such as balloons. Have your child plan as much of it as possible – make up the invitations, plan the music and games, even have a few nibbles and soft drinks.

It sounds a lot to organise but let them take the lead and be around to offer support where needed.

> *"I let my four-year old completely plan our family Boxing Day from deciding the menu to sorting out games and even the dress code. I was amazed with her ideas and her ability to plan and make lists (she sees me making to-do lists all the time!)"*
>
> Trusha, Mum and blogger at SecretStyleFile.com

Be a Happy News Journalist!

You will need: notepad and pen

It's easy to look at the headlines and feel that there isn't a lot of good news around – it rarely makes a top news story, yet there are lots of really positive things happening in communities.

Help your child look around your own local area to discover good news stories to report on – from fundraising efforts to supporting nature, see what you can find, then put together a small newspaper or newsletter reporting on it. This could be just for your own family and friends or circulate more broadly. It could become a regular publication over the Summer and beyond!

6

CAN-DO KINDNESS AND GIVING BACK

What does kindness mean to you? How can you demonstrate that to your children? Encouraging children to 'be kind' to others and to themselves is an essential part of a happy, healthy childhood.

Talk together about what kindness means, then draw a picture or write some words to express that, and display them in the house. Here are 20 suggestions for kindness and 'giving back' activities.

1. Wave hello to a neighbour
2. Write a letter to a friend or relative and post it to them
3. Donate pet supplies to a local rescue centre
4. Paint small rocks and leave around the neighbourhood
5. Pick up litter
6. Clear the dinner table without being asked
7. Take bubbles to the park and share with others
8. Grow 'help yourself herbs' leave them for passers-by
9. Make a bird seed feeder
10. Tidy your room without being asked
11. Give a sibling/other relative a hug
12 Ask for donations to charity instead of birthday presents
13. Leave seed packets outside for passers-by
14. Put a thank you note on the door for the postman
14. Tell a joke to make someone smile
15. Donate an item to the food bank
16. Pick flowers from the garden and give to a neighbour
17. Be kind to yourself
18. Sort out toys to donate to charity
19. Take a photograph and send it to a friend
20. Write a short story about kindness, and send to a friend

To help younger children understand about kindness, take a bowl of water, and drop very small objects into it, one at a time. Notice the ripple effect even from the tiniest of objects.

Talk about how just one small act of kindness such as smiling, or offering to help lay the table, can have a positive ripple effect on others.

As a child's social awareness increases, so does their awareness of the needs of others, and the ability to gain satisfaction from giving as well as receiving grows too. These foundational experiences can then be mapped on to a widening experience of a sense of community and mutual interests and obligations – first within the extended family, then later in the wider community.

Helping children understand how they can **add value in the world**, not just through their skills but also through kindness, is a fundamental part of nurturing a Can-Do child, supporting them to realise their potential, their hopes and dreams.

7

CAN-DO ECO AND OUTDOORS

Outdoor play provides both physical and mental health benefits, as well as a wonderful opportunity for children to appreciate nature and the environment. Active and free outside play also encourages greater independence, improves sensory skills, and helps connect with the outside world.

These activities support children's innate curiosity and creativity, and helps them learn about the wonder of nature, and ways to protect it.

Tree Wrapping

You will need: sticky back plastic paper

Whatever the season, choose a tree your child likes the look of and talk about what appealed to them about it. Then suggest 'wrapping' it up to make it look even more special, here's how:

- Using paper which is sticky on one side, wrap it around the tree trunk at a height your child can reach, making sure the sticky side is facing outwards.
- Now, go on a colour hunt, looking for anything safe and permissible to pick or collect and stick the items to the paper on tree. How many different colours and textures can they find?
- Now the tree is 'wrapped' in colours, talk about what they see, and create a story together.

Shadow Art

You will need: plain paper, toy animals (or whatever objects your child chooses), and a sunny day!

Place the paper on a flat surface outside and arrange the objects around the edge of the paper. As the shadows are cast, trace the shadows made. Create a fuller picture by adding in other details.

fingernailideas.com

Extend the activity by creating a shadow puppet theatre.

Ten Bottle Bowling

You will need: 10 empty plastic bottles; paint; sand; tennis ball

Add a little poster paint inside each of the 10 plastic bottles. Put the lid on and shake. Now add a little sand to each so they are weighted. Arrange the bottles into a 10-pin bowling formation, and with a tennis ball or similar, get bowling!

Add a twist to the traditional game by painting numbers on each bottle then either counting up the score based on the number of pins left standing, or those knocked down.

Nature's Numbers

You will need: chalk

Write out the numbers 1- 5 in chalk outside. The challenge is to find objects and place the correct amount of each on the right number. Use natural objects such as pinecones, leaves, pebbles, blades of grass, daisies. Turn this into a race by putting a time limit on, or add more numbers.

Be Plastic Clever

You will need: access to the internet

Take a look at the Kids Against Plastic web site, set up by children for children. It's packed full of ideas on how to become 'plastic clever' as well as outdoor ideas such as the *Pickup 1000* initiative.

There is also a great downloadable resource to help learn how to be more eco-friendly at home

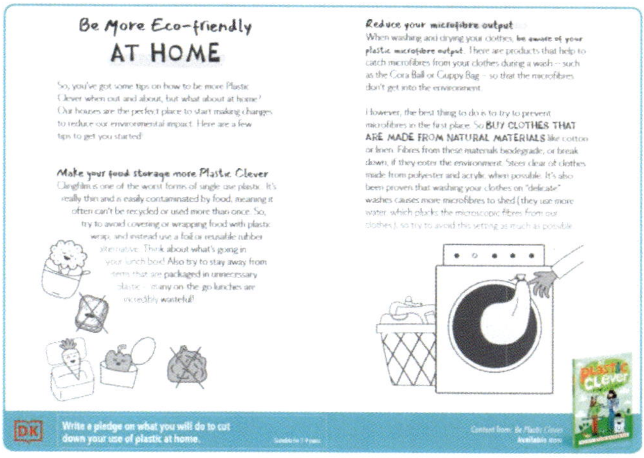

Be More Eco-friendly

AT HOME

So, you've got some tips on how to be more Plastic Clever when out and about, but what about at home? Our houses are the perfect place to start making changes to reduce our environmental impact. Here are a few tips to get you started!

Make your food storage more Plastic Clever

Clingfilm is one of the worst forms of single use plastic. It's really thin and is easily contaminated by food, meaning it often can't be recycled or used more than once. So, try to avoid covering or wrapping food with plastic wrap, and instead use a foil or reusable rubber alternative. Think about what's going in your lunch box! Also try to stay away from items that are packaged in unnecessary plastic – many on-the-go lunches are incredibly wasteful!

Reduce your microfibre output

When washing and drying your clothes, **be aware of your plastic microfibre output**. There are products that help to catch microfibres from your clothes during a wash – such as the Cora Ball or Guppy Bag – so that the microfibres don't get into the environment.

However, the best thing to do is to try to prevent microfibres in the first place. So **BUY CLOTHES THAT ARE MADE FROM NATURAL MATERIALS** like cotton or linen. Fibres from these materials biodegrade, or break down, if they enter the environment. Steer clear of clothes made from polyester and acrylic when possible. It's also been proven that washing your clothes on "delicate" washes causes more microfibres to shed (they use more water, which plucks the microscopic fibres from our clothes), so try to avoid this setting as much as possible.

DK

Write a pledge on what you will do to cut down your use of plastic at home.

Content from: Be Plastic Clever
Available now

Sticky Art

You will need: sticky back plastic (contact paper); tape

Find a suitable clear wall in the garden and tape the contact paper to it, making sure the sticky side is facing out. Using trial and error, let your child discover what sticks and what doesn't, to create their own piece of outdoor art in the garden.

Home-made Pizza Kits

You will need: basil seeds, plant pots or cut down clear plastic bottles, compost

Try this great idea as a gentle introduction to gardening. Make home-made pizza kits by firstly growing basil plants. You could use plastic plant pots, but even better cut down some empty clear plastic bottles, fill with compost, and add the seeds. These are great for watching the roots of the plant appear and grow, and recycling plastic! They take just a few weeks to grow 6cm or 8cm satisfying even the most impatient of gardeners! A home-made pizza kit includes:

- 1 x basil plant
- 1 x tortilla wrap
- 1 x recipe sheet (back of this book)

Taking the Tech Outdoors

You will need: smartphone; problem solving skills

There are some great family friendly ways to use technology outdoors, which focuses on teamwork, problem solving, and creativity, rather than being glued to a screen. Try these activities:

- *Geocaching* – a digital treasure hunt where everyone works together to follow co-ordinates and clues on a GPS/smartphone which lead to caches (small containers of hidden treasure)

- *Stargazing* – use one of the many free apps which have augmented reality to help learn about the stars and constellations, and how they can be used in navigation alongside GPS. Try re-creating the constellations using toothpicks and small marshmallows!

- *Go video* - create a video of your family outdoor adventures. Take it in turns to be in front and behind the camera, and share the end result with friends and family

Bringing the Outdoors In

You will need: paper plate; sticky back plastic (contact paper) thread; garden flowers

Give your child a bag or pot to collect flowers from the garden.

- Cut out two circular pieces of sticky back plastic (contact paper) just a little smaller than your paper plate, and put to one side
- Next cut the centre out of the paper plate
- Now stick the first piece of contact paper to the back of the plate so the sticky side faces upwards through the hole in the paper plate

- Stick the flowers onto the sticky paper
- Take the second circular piece of sticky backed plastic and place it over the top of the flowers to keep them in place
- Finally, make a small hole in the top of the paper plate from which you can add the thread and hang it in the window to catch the light

Older children could create smaller suncatchers using petals and leaves. Herbs are also a great way to aroma to the room where the suncatcher is hanging.

Treasure Hunts With A Twist

Treasure Hunts are enjoyed by children of all ages, but sometimes even the more traditional games benefit from a little twist. Try these ideas for treasure hunts with a difference:

- *Theme* your hunt according to interest e.g. Space, Fairies, Superheroes, Nature
- *Colour* – a hunt based around colours can help children learn about mixing colours too
- *Community* – ask questions about the local community which hunters then discover the answer to e.g. '*What type of ornament does No. 6 have in their front garden?*'
- *Sensory/Shape* – find items which represent the following: prickly, soft, rough, smooth and/or items which have points, are circular, triangular etc.
- *Create a series of QR codes* to hide around the house and/or garden. When scanned, each QR contains a clue to solve which leads to the next hidden QR and so on, until the final one reveals where the treasure is!
- *Indoors* – indoor hunts need a little more thought as the environment will be more familiar to your child, but use of cryptic clues can be fun and non-literal, promoting imaginative thinking

Eco-Bingo!

You will need: printed sheet at the back of this book

We can all do look after our planet, and that includes children now how matter young they are. **Using the sheet at the back of this book**, how many of the eco activities can your child complete over the holidays? Talk about how, as a family, you can all take action and what needs to be in place to help continue the good work.

ECO-BINGO!

Looking after the planet one small change at a time

Visit a **LOCAL** farmers market	Try to **FIX** something which is broken rather than throwing it away	Remember to take your **OWN BAGS** to the shops instead of buying more	Plant **BEE-FRIENDLY** flowers
Read a book about the environment	Hang clothes washing **OUTSIDE**	Turn the tap **OFF** when cleaning your teeth	For one week, only buy food which has **NO PACKAGING**
WALK on a short trip rather than going in the car	Take a **REUSABLE** water bottle with you when you go out	**DECIDE ON YOUR OWN ECO-ACTION**	Unplug electrical items not in use
Eat only **SEASONAL** food for a week	Make a meal from **LEFTOVERS**	Time your showers and aim to **REDUCE** by 1 minute every day for a week	Create something **USEFUL** from an item you would normally throw away
GROW your own edible plants such as herbs	Start a small **COMPOST** area in the garden	Sort out some toys you don't want and **DONATE** to charity	**TELL** your friends about Eco-Bingo!

Go on a Litter Pick

You will need: sensible shoes, gloves

Getting children involved in a litter pick is a fun way to keep your local community clean, and help your child learn about being responsible when it comes to rubbish, and its impact on the environment.

Introduce the litter pick by talking about what happens when the bin men arrive to take away the rubbish. A litter pick is great fun, gives an opportunity to meet other like-minded people.

You can turn it into a game to see who can fill their bag the fastest. Find your nearest tidy-up event at Keep Britain Tidy.

Spray the Shirt

You will need: fabric paint, spray bottles or water pistols, old t-shirt, cardboard

Place a piece of cardboard inside the t-shirt to stop the colours running through to the other side when the painting begins! Next, put a 3:1 mix of fabric paint and water into each spray bottle or water pistol and give it a good shake. Peg the t-shirt out on the washing line, making sure it's away from anything you don't want to get covered in paint. Get squirting or spraying!

Refill with as many colours as you have/like and remember to paint both sides of the t-shirt. Make sure the t-shirt fully dries before following the washing directions on the paint bottles.

8

LUCKY DIP BOREDOM BUSTERS

We hope you won't be hearing the words 'I'm Bored' too often over Summer, but we know children (of all ages!) will at some point decide there's really nothing for them to do.

The important thing to remember is that it's <u>absolutely fine</u> for your child to be bored – in fact we positively recommend it, and there's a lot of science to back up the benefits, including stimulating creativity, imagination, independence, and problem solving.

Scheduling something in for every day of the holidays can become quite stressful for parents too, so be sure to leave blank spaces on the holiday planner, giving children 'free play' time.

Just in case you need a little extra something up your sleeve, however, we've put together activity ideas for you to write out or print and cut out from the list below, pop them in a shoe box or pot with a 'lucky dip' label on the lid. Next time you hear those two words, direct your child to the lucky dip box for them to pick out an activity.

Make Your Own Word Search Game – use our template at the back of this book
Re-arrange your bedroom
Draw a self-portrait
Create a junk band and music from a bag of recyclable objects such as lids, rubber bands, empty bottles, cardboard, foil, balloons, empty tin cans, hair grips, pieces of polystyrene, tape, glue stick
Build something which floats
Watch a film and write a review of it afterwards
Cardboard canvas 1 - create something which moves from empty cardboard boxes e.g. marble run
Cardboard canvas 2 - create an object beginning with 'c' e.g. computer, cooker or any letter of the alphabet
Cardboard canvas 3 – build anything you like from empty cardboard boxes e.g. racetrack, market stall, washing machine, maze, castle or fort, puppet theatre, tv
Play board games
Play hide and seek
Visit Tate Kids to create art & technology, performance, cut and paste, paint and draw, sculpture, then upload your own work for the chance of it being displayed online
Create a story using the 'Pick a Story' cards at the back of this book

Draw a portrait of a person or animal in the house
Create a secret code and write notes for others to decipher
Play Rock Paper Scissors
Read a book
Create your own Top Trumps game based on an interest you have
Do a random act of kindness (see the list earlier in the book)
Make a maze from sticks and stones
What was it like when? Ask an elderly relative to tell you stories of when they were growing up, and record their memories to keep and pass on within the family
Start a scrapbook to record some of your favourite things you're doing over the Summer
Create your own Treasure Hunt
Have a picnic indoors
Have a picnic outdoors
Paint flowerpots
Make a picture from old bottle tops
Find an object which doesn't work anymore, take it apart and learn more about how things work, and how they go wrong
Go on a virtual tour of an exhibition anywhere in the world

Learn to sew – look for free online workshops for children
Cardboard shapes *(younger children)* – create shapes such as animals, people, cars from pieces of cardboard shapes. Decorate with stickers or colour them in
Mindful colouring-in
Invent something
Fly a Kite
Climb a tree
Create a comic strip
Write a poem

"Just letting the mind wander from time to time is important...for everybody's mental wellbeing and functioning. A study has even shown that, if we engage in some low-key, undemanding activity at same time, the wandering mind is more likely to come up with imaginative ideas and solutions to problems.

So, it's good for children to be helped to learn to enjoy just pottering – and not to grow up with the expectation that they should be constantly on the go or entertained." **Dr Teresa Belton**, Visiting Fellow, School of Education and Lifelong Learning, University of East Anglia

Photo: Can-Do Child Pinterest

9

PREPARING FOR RETURN TO SCHOOL

Before you know it, thoughts will turn to preparations for return to school after the holidays, or perhaps even starting school for the first time. Aside of the practical things such as getting feet measured, sorting uniforms, and choosing backpacks, how are you preparing your child for their return to school?

Children are usually excited to be going back to school, but they may be a little nervous too, wondering if anything has changed, whether they will make friends. Here are a few activities to help with that, along with some tips and tricks to discover how their first few days went without firing off 20 questions!

All About Me Bag

You will need: small paper bag

Give your child a small bag and get them to choose three or four things to put in it which they feel tells a story all about them, and what they've done over the summer. It could include something small they've made or coloured in, the wrapper from a favourite snack, an object in their favourite colour, or a photograph of family or a pet.

This bag gives your child confidence to talk about themselves to others, so encourage them to practice using it when talking to friends or relatives who might visit in the run up to school.

Back to School Bingo!

You will need: the sheet at the back of this book

Play Back to School bingo using the printout at the back of this book, as a fun way to make sure everything is ready for return to school. It can also act as a lead-in for conversations about anything your child is concerned about.
Depending on their age, your child may not need everything listed, so substitute with other things to talk about such as 'classroom'.

Simply cross off each one once your child is happy that they either have the item ready for school, or they know the information they need.

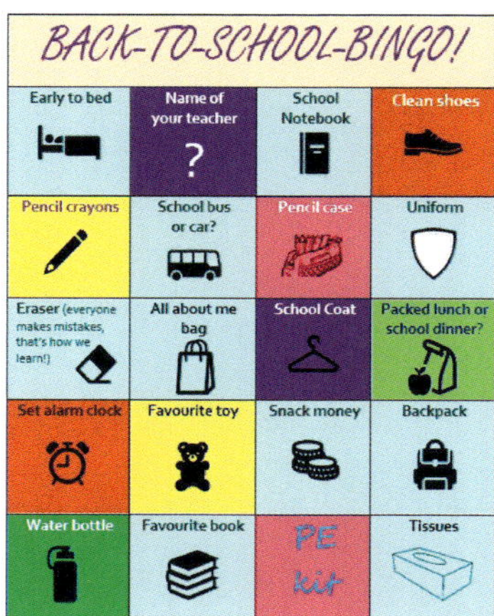

Something That Makes Me...

You will need: the sheet at the back of this book

Either on their own or with you, have your child complete the sheet available at the back of this book, about what makes them feel the different emotions listed, and talk about the things they can do when they feel those things e.g. dance
and clap when excited; talk to someone when they feel sad; take some time out when they feel angry.

When they have written on the sheet, talk through what kind of emotions they might be feeling about returning to or starting school, and keep the sheet handy for them to refer to.

Same Difference

You will need: to have communicated with school well before your child starts to complete this activity with them

Explore with your child **what is likely to have stayed the same** e.g. friends, uniform, journey to school, building etc. and **what might be different** such as a new teacher, classroom, or different subjects.
Balancing out the things which may have changed with those that haven't will provide reassurance for your child.

Countdown Calendar

You will need: a two-week calendar; small envelopes (optional)

Create an advent style calendar starting a couple of weeks before school starts. You could put a small surprise in a little envelope for each day e.g. a treat or words. The calendar will help children learn more about time, and create some excitement for when the return to school day arrives.

How Was School Today?

When your child returns from school, it's natural to want to know all about their day, but how to do this without asking the inevitable *'how was school today?'* often resulting in little or no information?

Here are 20 different ways to find out more about how your child's day went at school. Many of the questions have a natural follow-up such as 'Why was music your least favourite part?' just be careful not to fall into the 20 questions scenario again **- let your child take the lead in talking and give them space and time to reply.**

What was your favourite part of today?

What was your least favourite part?

What did you like best about your day today?

Was there anything that happened today that made you feel sad?

What was the most interesting thing you learnt in school today?

Is there anything you needed help with today?

What's the silliest thing that happened today?

If a spaceship came down and took someone from your class, who would it be?

Is there something you would have liked to have done differently today?

Is there someone at school you'd like to be friends with but aren't yet?

Tell me about a time you used your pencil today

Tell me about something that made you think hard today

Who were you kind to today?

Who was kind to you today?

Tell me about something which made you laugh today

Tell me something interesting your teacher has said today
What have you learnt today that you didn't know yesterday?

Who did you enjoy talking to the most today?

What are you looking forward to most tomorrow?

Is there a question you'd like me to ask you about school?

If your child is talking, try not to interrupt them, even if you're keen to understand more about what they've said. Wait for a natural end point then tell them *"I'd love to know more about that..."*

Try exploring feelings if you can, for example if your child talks about something that has happened to them at school but hasn't really said how they felt, encourage them to express their feelings by asking *"how did that make you feel?"* If they have trouble articulating their feelings use the cards from the 'Feeling Charades' game in the Health and Wellbeing section.

"Listen earnestly to anything [your children] want to tell you, no matter what. If you don't listen eagerly to the little stuff when they are little, they won't tell you the big stuff when they are big, because to them all of it has always been big stuff."
Catherine M Wallace

ABOUT THE AUTHOR

Lorraine Allman is a writer, educator, and international consultant with over 18 years' practical business experience working on a wide range of projects involving children and young people from early years through to school leavers.

She is author of numerous articles, and two books, most recently *'The Can-Do Child: Enriching the Everyday the Easy Way'* popular with both parents and teachers, presenting a child-centred approach to nurturing children's can-do potential through play using her unique Three Es' model of Engagement, Enterprise, and Enjoyment.

Lorraine works with organisations both in the UK and internationally to develop toolkits and programmes for nurturing a can-do mind and skills set in young people. She has developed an Enterprising and Life Skills programme for young learners in South Africa, and works with family centres and educators in UAE, supporting the annual 'Excellence in Early Years' conference for the MENA regions.

She chairs the judging panel for the *Young Enterprise Fiver* competition in UK Primary Schools, and delivers inspirational workshops to school children and University students. Lorraine works internationally through workshops, as well as digitally through apps and online training and resources. She is passionate about supporting parents to nurture can-do children, helping them grow up to be happy, resourceful, resilient, and confident individuals, achieving their full potential. She has one child, and lives in South East Wales.

You can read more about Lorraine's work at Can-Do Child at the back of this book.

PRINTABLES

You are welcome to photocopy the templates from the back of this book, or download the full A4 size versions of each at the following site www.candochild.com/download_resources.php for personal use only.

- Spot the Dots
- Book Bingo!
- Box the Dots
- Feeling charades cards
- Wheel of Choice
- Values Jar
- Would You Rather?
- Practical Skills for Life
- Home-made Pizza Kits
- Eco-Bingo!
- Word Search
- Pick a Story
- Back-to-school bingo!
- Something That Makes Me...

SPOT THE DOTS

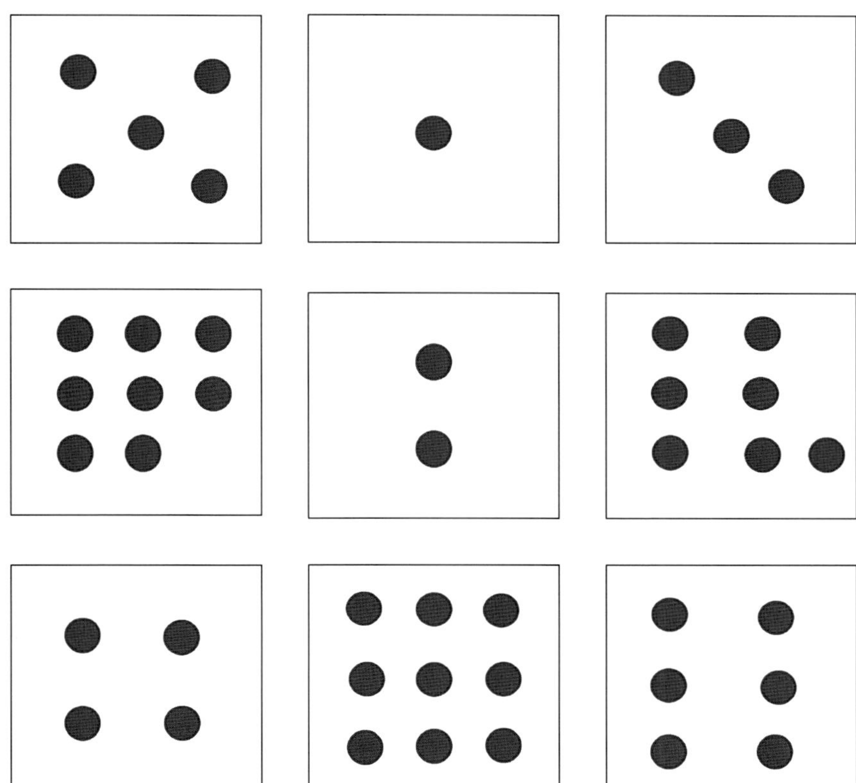

BOOK BINGO!

BOOK BINGO!			
Read in your **PYJAMAS**	Read to a **FRIEND** or relative	Read **3** days in a row	Find a **NEW WORD** in a book and learn what it means
Read a **NON-FICTION** book	Read in the dark with a **TORCH**	**SWAP** a book with someone-else	Read a book with a **NUMBER** in the title
Read **OUT LOUD**	Close your eyes and pick a book to read at **RANDOM**	Read a **POEM**	Read under the shade of a **TREE**
Listen to an **AUDIOBOOK**	Read on a **RAINY** day	Read in an **ACCENT**	Read a book which has an **ANIMAL** in the story
Measure your **TALLEST** book	Read a book that makes you **LAUGH**	Measure your **SHORTEST** book	Read sitting **NEXT to SOMEONE** who is also reading

BOX THE DOTS

FEELING CHARADES

Cut out each of the cards and put face down on the table. Take it in turns to pick one up and act out the emotion. Can the other player guess the emotion? If they can, they keep the card. Keep playing until all cards have been used.

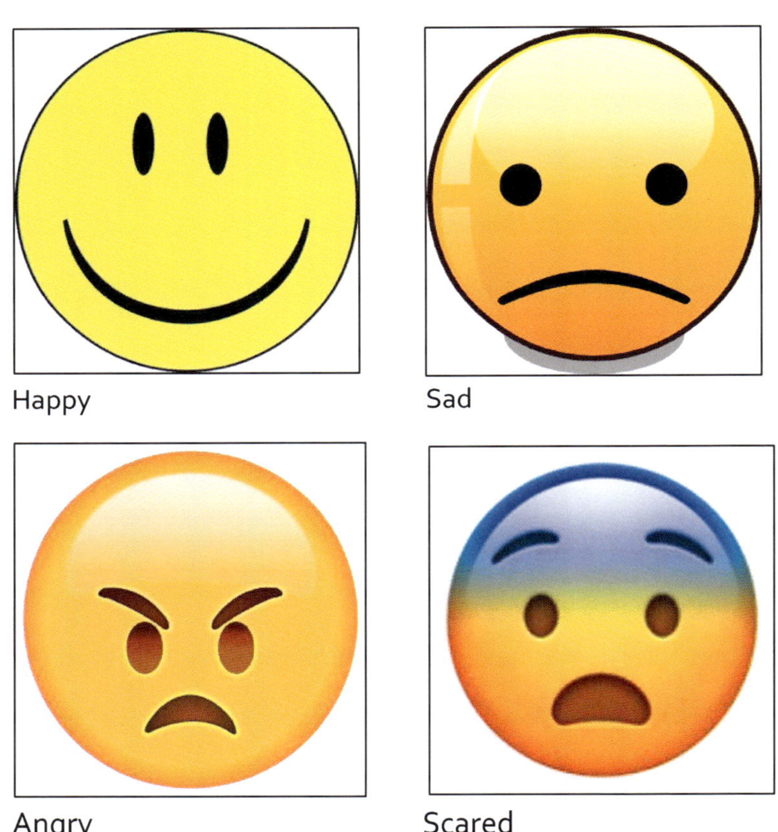

Happy

Sad

Angry

Scared

FEELING CHARADES cont'd...

Tired

Excited

Worried

Bored

WHEEL OF CHOICE

1. Cut out the wheel and arrow.
2. Glue both onto card, then glue the arrow at the bottom of the paper.
3. Push a split pin through the centre of the wheel.
4. Spin to find a solution your child is happy to try.

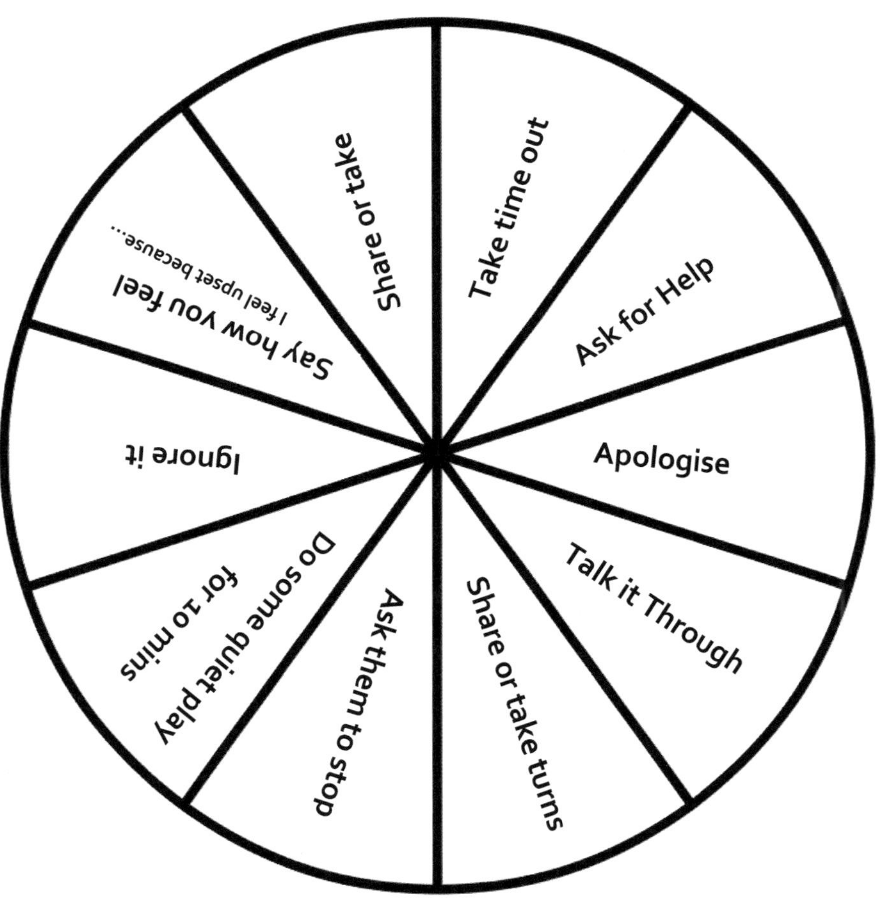

VALUES JAR

Cut out the 28 questions below, fold up, and place in an empty jar. Bring the jar out at family mealtimes or other occasions it feels right. Either one question is taken and read out for everyone to answer, or each person takes their own question and gives their answers, followed by supportive discussion.

What is your favourite word right now? Why?
Describe your perfect day
If you could have one superpower, what would it be?
What do you think is the most important job in the world?
Is it possible to help someone you've never met before?
Is it better to have too much of something, or not enough?
If you could only eat one meal a day, would it be breakfast, lunch, or tea?
If you could only eat just one thing for a year, what would it be?
What have you done today that was amazing?
How have you shown kindness today?
What is one thing you love about yourself?
If you could create one law that everyone had to follow, what would it be?
Name a skill you have that you could teach someone-else

What was the first thing you thought of when you woke up today?
What makes you laugh out loud?
If you could choose any animal as a pet what would it be? Why?
What is your favourite season? Why?
If you were stranded on a desert island, what would be the one thing you couldn't manage without?
Is there someone you'd like to be friends with but aren't at the moment?
What is your favourite room in your house? Why?
What is your favourite day of the week? Why
What is one thing you could have done better today?
What makes a happy family?
Is it every okay to cheat in exams/work/sports?
What is the best thing about school/work?
What is the hardest thing about school/work?
Has someone been kind to you today? How?
What is your least favourite household chore? Why?

WOULD YOU RATHER?

Would you rather... Be really fast, or really strong?	**Would you rather...** Be without the internet or the TV?	**Would you rather...** Have green hair or blue ears?
Would you rather... Be a tiger or a giraffe?	**Would you rather...** Swim or Surf?	**Would you rather...** Live in an igloo or a pyramid?
Would you rather... Play the trumpet or the drums?	**Would you rather...** Wear socks or shoes?	**Would you rather...** Have chocolate or chips?

WOULD YOU RATHER? cont'd...

Would you rather...

Have an extra finger or an extra toe?

Would you rather...

Eat a lemon or eat marmite?

Would you rather...

Have wings or wheels?

Would you rather...

Camp outside in Spring or Autumn?

Would you rather...

Be a magician or a superhero?

Would you rather...

Be famous for singing or dancing?

Would you rather...

Set the table for dinner or clear it up after?

Would you rather...

Sit in a bath of baked beans or a bath of rice pudding?

Would you rather...

Have an extra eye in the back of your head or an extra hand?

PRACTICAL SKILLS FOR LIFE

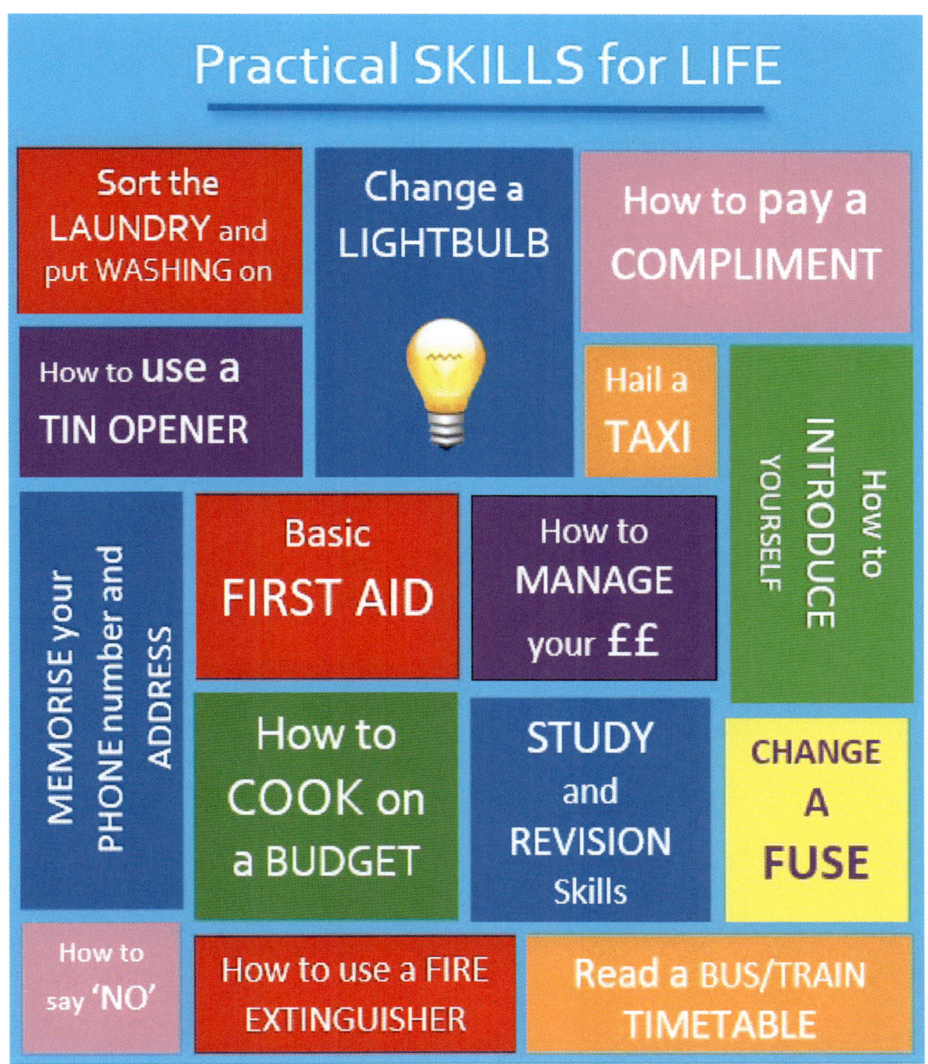

HOME-MADE PIZZA KIT RECIPE

1 x tortilla wrap
2 tbsp passata
Handful of grated cheese
Toppings as required
A little mozzarella cheese cut into thin slices
Handful of fresh basil leaves

1) Place the tortilla wrap on a baking tray and spread over 2tbsp of passata using the back of a spoon.

2) Sprinkle on a handful of grated cheese, toppings of your choice, and a little mozzarella.

3) Place the fresh basil leave around the pizza

4) Put in the oven for 6 minutes until the cheese starts to melt.

5) Remove and serve.

ECO-BINGO!

ECO-BINGO! *Looking after the planet one small change at a time*			
Visit a **LOCAL** farmers market	Try to **FIX** something which is broken rather than throwing it away	Remember to take your **OWN BAGS** to the shops instead of buying more	Plant **BEE-FRIENDLY** flowers
Read a book about the environment	Hang clothes washing **OUTSIDE**	Turn the tap **OFF** when cleaning your teeth	For one week, only buy food which has **NO PACKAGING**
WALK on a short trip rather than going in the car	Take a **REUSABLE** water bottle with you when you go out	**DECIDE ON YOUR OWN ECO-ACTION**	Unplug electrical items not in use
Eat only **SEASONAL** food for a week	Make a meal from **LEFTOVERS**	Time your showers and aim to **REDUCE** by 1 minute every day for a week	Create something **USEFUL** from an item you would normally throw away
GROW your own edible plants such as herbs	Start a small **COMPOST** area in the garden	Sort out some toys you don't want and **DONATE** to charity	**TELL** your friends about Eco-Bingo!

MY WORD SEARCH

MY WORD SEARCH

Find these words:

__________ __________ __________

__________ __________ __________

__________ __________ __________

PICK A STORY

Cut out the cards for each prompt and put into 3 separate bags – one each for character, setting, and object.

Pick one random card from each bag. With 16 cards in every bag there's no end of possible stories to create. You could also add in some of your child's small toys, or items from around the house.

CHARACTERS

PICK A STORY cont'd...

SETTINGS

PICK A STORY cont'd...

OBJECTS

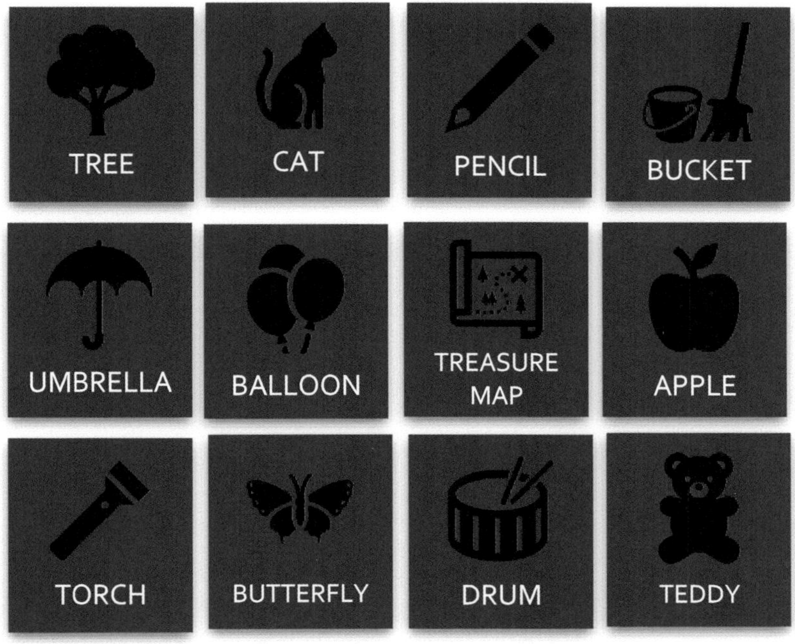

BACK-TO-SCHOOL BINGO!

Play Back to School bingo as a checklist to make sure everything is ready for return to school. It can also act as a lead-in for conversations about anything your child is concerned about.

Depending on their age, your child may not need all the items listed, so substitute with other things to talk about such as the classroom or subjects they will be learning.

Simply cross off each one once your child is happy that they either have the item ready, or they know the information.

SOMETHING THAT MAKES ME...

ABOUT CAN-DO CHILD®

Can-Do Child® supports parents and educators to help raise children with a can-do mindset who are happy, creative, resourceful, and resilient. It's a tried and tested play-based approach backed by professionals in the fields of early years, child development, parenting, child psychology, and education.

The range of resources available to parents and teachers are growing all the time, and currently include:

Can-Do Child app – packed full of activities focused on developing communication skills. Recommended by the *Good App Guide*.

Activity Cards – approved by the *Good Toy Guide* for ages 3-5 years and 5-7 years

Online course – *"Raising Can-Do Children: supporting your child to a happy, successful future"* 4.9* rating

The Can-Do Child® book – 100% 5* reviews on Amazon, recommended by parents and teachers

"Children don't come with a manual so the best way I have of supporting parents is to give them a toolbox and allow them to choose the right tools at the right time. For me, the way The Can-Do Child is being delivered provides parents with some really cool tools for their toolbox." **Dr Amanda Gummer,** UK's leading expert on play, play development, and child development.

Printed in Poland
by Amazon Fulfillment
Poland Sp. z o.o., Wrocław